D1038455

A Special Gift

For

From

Date

Grandchildren are a crown.

PROVERBS 17:6

Dedicated to
Grandma
Mamaw
Gran
Mimi
Grammy
Nana
Honey
Gammer
And all the other Grandmothers of the World.

Illustration Copyright © 2000, 2002 Debbie Mumm
www.debbiemumm.com

Text Copyright © 2000 The Brownlow Corporation
6309 Airport Freeway
Fort Worth, Texas 76117

All rights reserved. The use or reprinting of
any part of this book without the express written
permission of the publisher is prohibited.

ISBN 1-57051-485-2

Printed in China.

75 Ways to Spoil Your GRANDCHILD

Written by Caroline "Manaw" Brownlow

Illustrated by Debbie Mumm

Brownlow

Other Debbie Mumm Miniature Books

Little Treasures
Miniature Books

75 Ways to Be good to Yourself ❧ 75 Ways to Calm
Your Soul ❧ 75 Things to Do With a Friend ❧
75 Ways to Spoil Your Grandchild ❧
A Little Book of Love ❧
A Little Book for Tea Lovers ❧
Baby's First Little Book ❧ Baby Love Catch of the
Day ❧ Dear Teacher Friends ❧ The Gift of
Friendship Grandmother ❧ Happiness Is Homemade
Happy Birthday ❧ How to Be a Fantastic
Grandmother ❧ Love & Friendship ❧ Mom ❧
Sisters They Call It Golf

1. Hide candy on a low shelf in the kitchen (or your closet) that can be "found" each time your grandchild comes to visit.

2. Light sparklers on the 4th of July.

3. Save stale bread so that you can go to the park together and feed the duckies.

4. Overcome your fears - go down the slide with them rather than just watching from the safety of the ground.

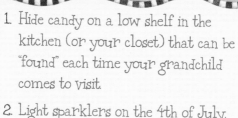

©Debbie Mumm

5. Play Candyland™ or other board games with them.

6. Play "Hide and Seek" in the house.

7. For older children, pick them up after school and treat them (and yourself) to an ice cream cone.

8. In the summer, eat watermelon together in the back yard and see who can spit the seeds the farthest.

9. Pray together before a meal or bedtime.

10. Pop popcorn together and eat it while watching their favorite show.

11. Keep a bottle of "bubbles" for blowing.

©Debbie Mumm

12. Take them camping. If you're not the outdoor type, a quilt tent in the living room will do. Don't forget the flashlight for reading stories and making shadow puppets.

13. Proudly display their "artwork" on the refrigerator.

14. Teach them how to "Eskimo kiss" by rubbing noses with you.

15. Have a toy box just for them to keep at Grandma's house.

16. Read Bible stories together. Always take time for pictures and questions.

17. Allow your grandchild to jump on your bed and sing "Five Little Monkeys."

Five little monkeys jumping on the bed.

One fell down and broke his head.

Mama called the doctor and the doctor said,

"No more monkeys jumping on the bed!"

Repeat with four, three, two, etc.

18. Buy videos that your grandchild likes and keep them at your house for rainy days.

19. Have a real tea party for granddaughters.

20. Take them to the zoo.

21. Buy animal crackers and eat them together.

22. Sing silly songs together.

23. Buy a kite and fly it together.

24. Make up stories to tell them when they sleep over.

25. Hold them in your lap and tell them how much you love them.

26. When they are old enough, take them on a trip ~ one grandchild at a time.

27. Carve a pumpkin together in the autumn.

28. Always keep popsicles in the freezer.

29. Plant seeds together in the spring and watch them grow.

30. At Christmas time, tell them the story of the first Christmas.

FEATHERED NEST

• ROCK • A • BYE • BABIES •

31. Take them to an historical place and teach them what happened there.

32. Write a special letter to them (while they are a baby) to be read at their wedding.

33. Tell them about the day they were born.

34. Tell stories about their mother or father when they were young.

35. Bake sugar cookies together and decorate with "sprinkles." Cut out lots of different shapes for added fun.

36. Buy a rubber ducky for your bathtub. Let them play with it when you're not.

37. Go on a picnic together and play games.

RUBBER · DUCKY

38. Go to a pet store and look at the baby animals together ~ just remember not to make a purchase without the express written consent of the parents.

GOOD BOY

CHOW

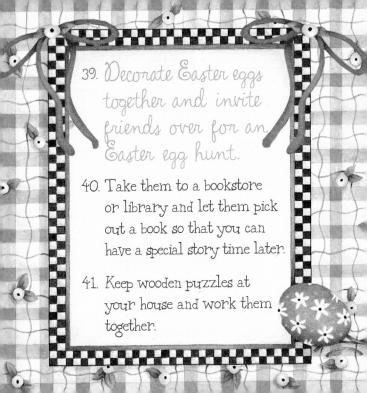

39. Decorate Easter eggs together and invite friends over for an Easter egg hunt.

40. Take them to a bookstore or library and let them pick out a book so that you can have a special story time later.

41. Keep wooden puzzles at your house and work them together.

42. Let them play on your computer.

43. Bake cookies together and deliver them to special friends just for fun.

44. Make snow ice cream together. (Snow, sugar, milk and vanilla)

45. Go to a horse farm and ride ponies.

46. Keep an extra pair of "jammies" at Grandma's house.

47. Bake a pie together, making a "miniature" one just for them.

48. Buy a cute greeting card for them and write a special note in it. Send it in the mail ~ even if you live in the same town.

49. Play "horsey". You be the horse and teach them to say, "Giddy~up, Grandma."

50. Teach them how to peel an orange, and then eat it together.

51. In the summertime, hook up an old~fashioned water sprinkler and run through it together.

52. Give them one special Christmas ornament each year until they turn 18. Then they will have a wonderful collection of Grandma's love to decorate their own tree.

53. Take a train ride together ~ if only to the next town.

54. Teach them to say, "My Grandma loves me."

55. Go outside at night, look at the moon together and teach them this poem:

"I see the moon, the moon sees me
God made the moon
and God made me."

56. Make a scrapbook to give to them on their eighteenth birthday.

57. Tell them stories of your childhood.

58. Ask them to sleep over and cook animal-shaped pancakes in the morning.

59. Watch cartoons together.

60. Always attend their recitals, school plays and athletic events.

61. Take them out to eat at a restaurant of their choice.

62. Go to the movies together.

63. Go to the mall and have your picture taken together in an instant picture booth. Make funny faces and laugh a lot.

64. Tell them how much God loves them.

65. Make something hand-made just for them.

66. Really listen to your grandchild when they talk to you.

67. Buy a goldfish bowl and a goldfish to care for. Give the fish a special, silly name.

68. Call your grandchild on the phone just to talk.

69. Keep balloons to blow up and play with.

70. Teach them how to jump. This will be a big help later in learning activities such as hopscotch, jump rope, and leapfrog.

71. Play ball in the back yard.

GRANDMA'S CLOSET

72. Roast hot dogs and marshmallows over a grill, campfire or fireplace.

73. Collect inexpensive items for "dress-up" and keep them in a special box, drawer or closet just for them

74. Keep a special cookie jar filled with their favorite cookies.

75. Tell them that they do not have to do anything to earn your love. Tell them that you love them just because they are your grandchild.